The Humanities, Higher Education, and Academic Freedom
Three Necessary Arguments

Michael Bérubé
Professor of Literature, Pennsylvania State University, USA

and

Jennifer Ruth
Associate Professor in English, Portland State University, USA

palgrave
macmillan

First published 2015 by
PALGRAVE MACMILLAN

Palgrave Macmillan in the UK is an imprint of Macmillan Publishers Limited, registered in England, company number 785998, of Houndmills, Basingstoke, Hampshire RG21 6XS.

Palgrave Macmillan in the US is a division of St Martin's Press LLC, 175 Fifth Avenue, New York, NY 10010.

Palgrave Macmillan is the global academic imprint of the above companies and has companies and representatives throughout the world.

Palgrave® and Macmillan® are registered trademarks in the United States, the United Kingdom, Europe and other countries.

ISBN 978–1–137–50610–8   hardback
ISBN 978–1–137–50611–5   paperback

This book is printed on paper suitable for recycling and made from fully managed and sustained forest sources. Logging, pulping and manufacturing processes are expected to conform to the environmental regulations of the country of origin.

A catalogue record for this book is available from the British Library.

A catalog record for this book is available from the Library of Congress.

Typeset by MPS Limited, Chennai, India.

low cost to the individual student and his or her family. The result of this synthesis was freedom to choose a field of study without overriding awareness of its future income potential. A further result was graduation with little to no debt, allowing the graduate from a low-income background to have the same shot as others at the freedom to take poorly paying but satisfying work, or a shot at international travel, or a shot at being a professional painter or dancer.[13]

Newfield is right about the culture wars, and right about privatization; the only thing missing from his otherwise brilliant analysis of how the defunding of public universities constituted an assault on the American middle class is an acknowledgment that despite it all, undergraduates keep dreaming of being professional painters and dancers, as the numbers of majors in the fine and performing arts show us. It is odd, is it not? Why, one would almost be tempted to conclude that the arts—and, to a lesser degree, the humanities—have some intellectual, creative, and emotional power after all.

And so the obvious question asserts itself: if the numbers are so much less alarming than we've been led to believe, why do scholars and teachers in the humanities continue to talk—persistently, strenuously, even obsessively—in terms of "crisis"?

There are two reasons, we think. One is that there are plenty of scholars and teachers in the humanities who have been inured to the idea that they are being systemically ignored, misunderstood, and/or devalued. This is understandable enough; they walk across campus and see the gleaming new Business Administration building, the sparkling, beautifully equipped Center for Nanotechnology and Advanced Bioengineering, and the gorgeous new stadium, arena, and student activity center—and then they trudge into their ancient cubicle in the dilapidated, un-air-conditioned Arts and Humanities Building, and they grumble to themselves about campus priorities. Or, depending on their temperament, they take a perverse comfort in their place at the bottom of the funding food chain, telling themselves that people just don't appreciate the finer things in life, such as the study of the monuments and artifacts of human civilization—worth more, ultimately, than any amount of filthy lucre or creature comforts. These people are a ready audience for the "decline of the humanities" narrative, because it confirms for them what they are already wont to believe: they are surrounded by philistines, Know-Nothings, and annoying businessmen from Porlock.

For most professors, though, it is not resentment or self-pity that makes the decline narrative so compelling. It is the fact that the narrative *feels right*, inasmuch as it attempts to account for the pervasive, sinking feeling that something is very much amiss. Among humanities professors and graduate students, there is a keen sense that even if there is no immediate crisis of undergraduate enrollment, there nonetheless is a crisis. It is a crisis of graduate education and professional employment, and though it is not confined to the humanities—it is now endemic to higher education in general—it is often felt to be most pronounced in the humanities. It is also, relatedly, a crisis of funding, of prestige, and of legitimation. And whether this crisis is experienced as disorganized malaise or diamond-tipped rage depends largely on the person's employment situation. Because the crisis is not one of disappearing students. It is one of disappearing tenure-track jobs. Too many people have been snookered into thinking that the jobs disappeared because the students did; we have written this book to put that canard to rest once and for all.

* * *

We believe ours is something more than the standard-issue "defense" of the humanities, or of the liberal arts tradition in higher education more generally (which would of course include the physical and social sciences—everything that is not a narrowly designed "vocational" program). The book is partly that, particularly in the following chapter, but we think there are enough of those out there. Helen Small's *The Value of the Humanities*, to take one example, offers a painstakingly careful and measured assessment of the genre. We believe that the real crisis is that the profession of college teaching has been drastically deprofessionalized over the past 40 years, and that college teachers need to find ways of making this case to the general public—without suggesting that the legions of teachers off the tenure track are not doing professional-quality teaching. We want to explain to people who may not know what a provost is, or who don't use the word "decanal" in conversation, what *this* crisis looks like.

So what are these "three necessary arguments" of our subtitle? They go something like this. The first two are familiar in some precincts of the academy, but not all—and very rarely get an adequate hearing outside. The third is wholly unacknowledged, and sheds new and disturbing light on the first two.

One, the humanities are in fine shape, insofar as their intellectual value is concerned. We don't agree with every last thing every single person in the humanities has written or said over the past 40 years, but on the whole, the disciplines of the humanities are home to exciting and ambitious work in both emerging and traditional fields.

Two, while all this exciting and ambitious work has been going on, the profession of college teaching has been hollowed out as full-time, tenure-track positions have been converted to highly precarious positions (both full-time and part-time) that offer no possibility of tenure—which means, basically, all the job security of Wal-Mart or McDonald's.

Three, the deprofessionalization of college teaching has had consequences with which no one has fully come to terms—in academe or out. These consequences have unsettling implications for the future of graduate programs and for the mundane but important business of running academic departments. They are complex and contradictory and hard to fix, and we will elaborate on them in Chapters 2 and 3; suffice it to say here that massive hiring off the tenure track has effectively foregone systems of professional review for college faculty.

Here's how these three arguments came together. In the middle of the summer of 2013, as I was wading through the latest spate of decline-of-the-humanities essays, Jennifer wrote to me on what might seem to be an unrelated matter: a policy statement from the American Association of University Professors, recommending that all "contingent" faculty (we will explain the terminology, which is surprisingly complicated; for now we will use "contingent" to designate everyone not on the tenure track) be included in campus governance. The policy is a strong attempt to address a dire situation: at many universities, contingent faculty have no say whatsoever in any aspect of the way their departments or campuses are governed, so they are subject to potentially capricious hiring (and firing) practices. However, as Jennifer pointed out, since we are talking about faculty who effectively have no academic freedom—who can be punished or fired for any reason, usually without recourse to appeal or review—it is problematic to argue that they should serve on committees where their opinions and comments may well alienate the person or persons who hired them. Jennifer knew that I am an advocate for the rights of contingent faculty, and that (alongside my interest in disability studies) I focused my year as president of the Modern Language Association on their working conditions—even though the president of the MLA, and the MLA more generally, has nothing more than a bully pulpit when it comes to the working conditions of contingent faculty.

This conversation was punctuated by a series of essays that Jennifer wrote for the well-regarded academic blog *Remaking the University*, run by Michael Meranze and Christopher Newfield.[14] And at some point, I realized that I was corresponding with a former department chair who had actually reversed the trend toward the casualization of academic labor in her own department; who had successfully fought for tenure-track lines and successfully undone some of the under-the-table deals enjoyed by some of her faculty; and who was writing important essays about the experience. Asking her to co-author this book was an easy call.

For the most part, my experience has been that of an advocate in national organizations, though I have worked on my own workplace, as well. I helped rewrite the bylaws of the Penn State English department not long after my arrival in 2001, to ensure that our non-tenure-track faculty could not be capriciously demoted or fired, and that they had recourse to regular reviews as well as an appeal process when they disagreed with a review. I also serve on the Faculty Senate at Penn State, having been elected in 2012. But other than that, my experiences in this wing of academe consist mostly of my work with the national AAUP, leading two investigations of universities closing programs and firing tenured faculty, and writing a report on the role of the faculty in conditions of financial exigency. And, of course, writing essays and giving talks about the state of the humanities. Jennifer, by contrast, has done the critical but almost always invisible work of running a department, negotiating with deans and provosts, coming to terms with the stubborn fact that we have evolved a two- or three-tier hiring system in academe: one tier involves national searches, careful vetting processes, and rigorous peer review. The other two are almost entirely ad hoc, involving short- and long-term contingent faculty hired (and fired) almost any old way. The short-term faculty are often referred to as "adjuncts," and we will employ that designation here, differentiating them from the long-term, full-time faculty off the tenure track—but considering both groups as "contingent" faculty.

Jennifer and I decided on the following division of labor: we each would write on the state of the profession as we have seen and experienced it. Sometimes our voices are combined, and sometimes they are distinct. We hope that for the most part, *who* is talking *when* will be clear and that the pronoun shifts are not distracting. (The order of our names below the chapter titles in the Introduction, Chapters 3 and 4 shows who wrote most of it. Michael wrote Chapter 1 solo and Jennifer wrote Chapter 2. In Chapter 4, we hand the baton back and forth, and indicate when we are doing so.) Before we get to the nuts and bolts of what has gone wrong in the academic labor system—and how to set about fixing it—I take one more chapter to address the actual substance of work in the humanities in the past few decades. Too often, when I have rebutted the enrollment argument, I have been met with complaints that the numbers aren't really the point—the point is the sorry state of humanities departments in the United States, filled as they are with second-rate ideologues and incomprehensible cliques. I do not want that complaint to go unaddressed, not least because I have a visceral intolerance for second-rate ideologues and incomprehensible cliques. I just don't agree that American humanities departments are filled with them. I do, however, agree that the explicitly political attacks on humanities departments, over the past few decades, have helped to delegitimate new work in the humanities—precisely as they were designed to do. We then concentrate on the crisis of deprofessionalization—what it looks like from the inside, what it means for higher education, and how we can begin to turn it around. Chapter 2 is Jennifer's, and everything else is both of us, with some single-voiced sections scattered throughout. The Appendix consists of recommendations Jennifer and her colleague Amy Greenstadt have proposed for transitioning Portland State to a majority tenure-track professoriate, and that we think can be generalized well beyond Portland State.

Now a few words about what we hope to do in this book and why. The employment situation in academe is this: contingent-faculty members now make up over one million of the 1.5 million people teaching in American colleges and universities—about 70 percent of all faculty. Many of them are working at or under the poverty line, with an average salary of about $2700 per

14

Professors was founded one hundred years ago. And in the following chapter, we'll give you some specific reasons why the humanities are central to that mission.

Notes

1. David Brooks, "The Humanist Vocation," *New York Times* 20 Jun. 2013: A23.
2. William M. Chace, "The Decline of the English Department," *American Scholar* (Autumn 2009). http://theamericanscholar.org/the-decline-of-the-english-department/
3. Mark Bauerlein, "English's Self-Inflicted Wounds," *Chronicle of Higher Education* 31 May 2013. http://chronicle.com/blogs/conversation/2013/05/31/englishs-self-inflicted-wounds/
4. MSNBC.com no longer carries that report in its online archive, but I discussed it at the time at the blog Crooked Timber. See Michael Bérubé, "Breaking News: Humanities in Decline! Film at 11," 16 Nov. 2010. http://crookedtimber.org/2010/11/16/breaking-news-humanities-in-decline-film-at-11/
5. The most egregious offenders were Alvin Kerman and John M. Ellis. See Kernan, *The Death of Literature* (New Haven: Yale University Press, 1992) and, as editor, *What's Happened to the Humanities?* (Princeton University Press, 1997); Ellis, *Literature Lost: Social Agendas and the Corruption of the Humanities* (New Haven: Yale University Press, 1997) and "Poisoning the Wells of Knowledge," *New York Times* 28 Mar. 1998.
6. Andrew Delbanco, "The Decline and Fall of Literature," *New York Review of Books* 4 Nov. 1999. http://www.nybooks.com/articles/archives/1999/nov/04/the-decline-and-fall-of- literature/
7. Frank Kermode, "The Academy vs. the Humanities," *Atlantic Monthly* Aug. 1997. http://www.theatlantic.com/past/docs/issues/97aug/academy.htm
8. Nate Silver, "As More Attend College, Majors Become More Career-Focused," *New York Times* 25 Jun. 2013. http://fivethirtyeight.blogs.nytimes.com/2013/06/25/as-more-attend-college-majors-become-more-career-focused
9. Ben Schmidt, "A Crisis in the Humanities?" *Chronicle of Higher Education* 10 Jun. 2013. http://chronicle.com/blognetwork/edgeofthewest/2013/06/10/the-humanities-crisis/
10. See *The Teaching of the Arts and Humanities at Harvard College: Mapping the Future*, p. 7. http://artsandhumanities.fas.harvard.edu/files/humanities/files/mapping_the_future_31_may_2013.pdf

11. Verlyn Klinkenborg, "The Decline and Fall of the English Major," *New York Times* 22 Jun. 2013. http://www.nytimes.com/2013/06/23/opinion/sunday/the-decline-and-fall-of-the-english-major.html?_r=0

12. Christopher Newfield, *Unmaking the Public University: The Forty-Year Assault on the Middle Class* (Cambridge, MA: Harvard University Press, 2008), p. 268.

13. Newfield, *Unmaking*, p. 270.

14. See Jennifer Ruth, "When Tenure-Track Faculty Take on the Problem of Adjunctification," *Remaking the University* 25 May 2013. http://utotherescue.blogspot.com/2013/05/when-tenure-track-faculty-take-on.html; "Why Are Faculty Complicit in Creating a Disposable Workforce?," *Remaking the University* 13 Jul. 2014. http://utotherescue.blogspot.com/2014/07/why-are-faculty-complicit-in-creating.html; and "What Can We Do Now that Adjunct Sections are Written Into Universities' Fiscal Survival Strategy?," *Remaking the University* 22 Jul. 2014. http://utotherescue.blogspot.com/ 2014/07/what-can-we-do-now-that-adjunct.html

15. Stacey Patton, "The Ph.D. Now Comes with Food Stamps," *Chronicle of Higher Education* 6 May 2012. http://chronicle.com/article/From-Graduate-School-to/131795/

16. David Laurence, "A Profile of the Non-Tenure-Track Academic Workforce," *ADE (Association of Departments of English) Bulletin* 153 (2014), pp. 6–22.

17. See Daniel Kovalik, "Death of an Adjunct," *Pittsburgh Post-Gazette* 18 Sept. 2013. http://www.post-gazette.com/opinion/Op-Ed/2013/09/18/Death-of-an-adjunct/stories/201309180224, and L. V. Anderson, "Death of a Professor," *Slate* 17 Nov. 2013. http://www.slate.com/articles/news_and_politics/education/2013/11/death_ of duquesne_adjunct_margaret_mary_vojtko_what_really_happened_to_her.html

18. Edward H. Levi, *Point of View: Talks on Education* (University of Chicago Press, 1970), p. 170.

19. Levi, *Point of View*, p. 169.

contingent and cultural character of the existing conventions governing the scope of universality does not deny the usefulness or importance of the term "universal." It simply means that the claim of universality has not yet received a full or final articulation and that it remains to be seen how and whether it will be articulated further.[8]

To this I can only say, *well, what did you expect?* Of course the universal may be defined differently in the future, and of course we don't know what form it will take. Indeed, the idea that the universal could ever receive a "full and final articulation" seems to me nonsensical: you have to imagine a future world in which all humans agree on the meaning of the term "universal," and we all congratulate each other on finally getting *that* settled. When you put it that way, it sounds kind of preposterous. It might even involve a children's theme park located at the symbolic (and cheerful) border of Israel and the Republic of Palestine.

But strange as it may sound, one of the leading contemporary defenders of the Enlightenment *did* put it that way. Jürgen Habermas was the *bête noire* of the academic left in the 1980s and 1990s not merely because he called Foucault and Derrida "young conservatives"[9] in the course of defending "the project of modernity" (that is, Enlightenment) but especially because he construed the "ideal speech situation" as free from domination (which is good) and oriented toward consensus (which is bad). Jean-François Lyotard's reply that consensus is "terror" was beyond hyperbolic, but surely there were and are very good reasons to object to a theory of communication that takes consensus as its a priori goal. As I noted in *What's Liberal about the Liberal Arts?*, my graduate students have all learned to reject Habermas and embrace his critics (thereby provoking the question of how they managed to achieve such a consensus), whereas my undergraduates don't see anything wrong with the idea that people should try to communicate in order to achieve reciprocal recognition and consensus. But here, the point needs to be made, on Habermas's behalf, that reciprocal recognition is not the same thing as consensus; I can understand you (or try to) without agreeing with what you say. And the point needs to be conceded, *pace* Habermas, that establishing consensus as the orientation of communication *is* coercive: it's like imagining all of culture and society as a form of jury duty, and political debate as juror deliberation. We don't get to go home until we all agree: *that* will be our full and final articulation.

There are other problems with Habermas, as well: his emphasis on reason has seemed to some critics to set emotion and affect at a discount, though one can plausibly counterargue, as Amanda Anderson has done, that there are a variety of ways to understand and achieve reciprocal recognition, not all of which rely exclusively on communicative reason.[10] But in the end, I think it is better to conceive of Enlightenment universalism as an incomplete project than to dismiss it as an illegitimate one (or to claim, as Lyotard did, that the Enlightenment leads directly to the Holocaust). And the reason I think so has everything to do with my reading of Butler's critique of universalism. That critique, as I see it, launches three ultimately incompatible claims: one, that the universal gains its meaning from decidedly less-than-universal cultural conditions of its articulation; two, that some claims to universality are partial and exclusionary, and need to be more universal; three, that the universal has not received a full and final articulation. The first two claims are in tension with one another, and the first may in fact undercut the second: that is, if you grant that the universal is always articulated as the less-than-universal, it's not clear that you can fault human rights groups for having a less than universal conception of universal rights. But it's the third claim I want to focus on now, because it suggests that *the universal can always be called to account, called into question.* Universalism in these terms appears attractive to me precisely because it announces a promise whose fulfillment can never be fully and finally achieved: it does not dictate norms (despite the widespread conflation of universalism with normative theory), it does not premise equality on sameness (with regard to race, gender, sexuality, or disability), but it does say that you can always debate whether a universalist principle is sufficiently universal.

To take a parallel example from work closer to my own, in disability studies rather than queer theory: the promise announced by universalism is what motivates Eva Kittay's disability-rights critique of the social contract tradition from John Locke to John Rawls—yet another Enlightenment project. Kittay's argument in *Love's Labor*, which is picked up and elaborated in Martha Nussbaum's *Frontiers of Justice*, is that the idea of the social contract, in which "free, equal, and independent" parties form societies for "mutual advantage" (and, in Rawls's terms, establish the principles of justice from behind a "veil of ignorance" so as not to tilt the scales to their own benefit), will always exclude people with significant intellectual disabilities, who are not free, equal, and independent and cannot offer their fellow citizens the possibility of mutual advantage. Though Rawls addresses disability in what he calls the "legislative phase" of the deliberations over justice, Kittay and Nussbaum are right to see that the exclusion of people with intellectual disabilities from the foundations of justice is intrinsic to the social-contract tradition. (As Adolph Reed, Jr. has put it in another context, this is a form of "I'll come back for you" politics.) Thus even Rawls's aspiration to a universal theory of justice, in which (for example) the Rawlsian Difference Principle permits inequalities in the distribution of goods only if those inequalities benefit the least-well-off, is weighed in disability studies' version of the scales of justice and found wanting, because its form of universalism is not universal enough.

And here's the most important point. *Only* a universalist theory is open to this kind of critique; no one can plausibly critique the theory of the divine right of kings or the great chain of being for being exclusionary or hierarchical. They're meant to be; they are impervious to egalitarian challenges. If however you advance a principle as universalist, a principle that makes that open-ended promise, you are obliged to admit all comers and take on all challenges, from anyone and everyone who believes that your claim to universalism isn't sufficiently universalist. That, finally, is why I'm ultimately with Habermas (and Thurgood Marshall) in the belief that modernity is an incomplete project. The study of disability, and the history of disability, has led me to believe that only the promise of universalism holds out the hope for an adequately capacious understanding of humans and the humanities.

* * *

Now, if I may, let me turn for a moment and say a few words about my own work in this relatively new field, and why I think it matters as a branch of the humanities.

Ten or 12 years ago, I was talking with Eva Kittay, and we were complaining to each other that philosophy had so little to say on the subject of disability—except, of course, when philosophers were finding reasons why people with intellectual disabilities do not meet their standards for entities entitled to something called human dignity. So for some years now, I've been in the position of saying to my colleagues in philosophy, "your silence with regard to cognitive disability is most dismaying," followed in short order by "actually, your undervaluation of the lives of people with cognitive disabilities is even more dismaying. I liked you all better when you were silent." Since I have an adult son with an intellectual disability, this is personal for me in various ways—but it is also a challenge for the humanities more broadly, as well. I will elaborate on one of those ways, because it will highlight nicely the difference between theories about humans that are open to endless egalitarian challenge and theories that are not.

In his 1994 book, *Rethinking Life and Death*, Peter Singer famously claimed that "to have a child with Down syndrome is few decades that we simply do not know what the range of functioning looks like, and therefore do not rightly know what to expect. Because what has changed about Down syndrome in the last 50 years? Not the biology—not the chromosomal nondisjunction that gives people with Down syndrome an extra twenty-first chromosome. That is precisely what it has always been—a major error during meiosis. What *has* changed are the social policies and social practices through which we understand Down syndrome—and, if you will, through which we "administer" Down syndrome. That is the real challenge of being a parent of a child with Down syndrome: it's not just a matter of contesting other people's low expectations of your child, it's a matter of recalibrating your own expectations time and time again—not only for your own child, but for Down syndrome itself.

For who could have imagined, just 40 or 50 years ago, that the children we were institutionalizing and leaving to rot could in fact grow up to become actors? (I mention acting not because it's the *ne plus ultra* of human achievement but because it requires a level of self-awareness and self-fabrication that no one would have thought possible for people with Down syndrome a generation ago.) I take issue with Singer's passage, then, not because I'm a sentimental fool or because I believe that one child's surprising accomplishments and observations suffice to win the argument, but because as we learn more about Down syndrome, we honestly don't know what constitutes a "reasonable expectation" for a person with Down syndrome.

More than this, I take issue with one of Singer's central premises—one that is shared by philosopher Jeff McMahan: namely, the belief that cognitive capacity is an index of one's moral status as a being. This belief is tied strongly to—in fact, serves as the basis of—Singer and McMahan's advocacy of animal rights. Singer insists that the only secular reason humans can endow themselves with rights that they deny to animals is that we base those rights on our superior cognitive abilities (that is, those of us who do not base them on our possession of immortal souls). Mere species membership alone is insufficient, for Singer and for McMahan, as a basis for distinguishing ourselves from animals; that is "speciesism," and they regard it as analogous to racism. (It is a terrible analogy, if you stop to think for a moment about the difference between interracial sex and interspecies sex—a difference only the most troglodyte racist would seek to elide.) Indeed, Singer argues that if he is making his argument to a rational alien who understands him, he therefore has more in common with that alien than he does with a human being with significant intellectual disabilities:

> if it happens that one of you is an alien who has cleverly disguised yourself in a human shape, but you are capable of understanding this argument, I am talking to you just as I am talking to members of my own species. In important respects, I have much more in common with you than I do with someone who is of my species but, because he or she is profoundly mentally retarded, has no capacity for verbal communication with me at all.[12]

This is not funny stuff. It is, frankly, horrific. And yet the comic possibilities must be remarked. I seized upon one of them at the conference at which Singer presented this paper, and announced during the group photo that I am indeed a sentient alien in human shape, and do not see any basis for Singer's belief that he has anything important in common with me. One might also adduce Kent Brockman, the anchorman from *The Simpsons*, who, when he believes that the space shuttle has been taken over by giant space ants, famously announces, "and I for one welcome our new insect overlords! I'd like to remind them that as a trusted TV personality I could be helpful in rounding up others to toil in their underground sugar caves!" Or one might adduce the renowned "To Serve Man" episode of *Twilight Zone*, imagining a tall, smiling, telepathic alien being who is touched an attempt to avoid the trap of generating SCH cheaply for the university. ("We will grow SCH," we said, "but not through contingent appointments.") In our minds, the costs we were paying were small next to the prospect of more good jobs and fewer bad jobs in the department.

At the time I was surprised that people didn't see things the way we did. When I think back now to the fist-fights my brother and I had over whose turn it was to feed the dog or the period after our first daughter's birth when my husband and I were wrestling to make sure that the other spouse pulled precisely 50 percent of the parenting weight, I understand better what we were up against. As every sibling, spouse, department chair, union organizer, and university administrator knows, struggles over divisions of labor are rarely pretty.

The consolation we have is that it worked. By making clear that we would not continue to grow on the backs of contingent faculty, my colleagues and I got permission for two new tenure lines and an agreement to convert a fixed-term position when someone retired into a tenure-track position. Within two years, we had three new tenure lines that were not merely replacements for retiring tenure-track faculty. Further, during a period of budget cuts when replacement searches in other departments were being canceled (and the lost SCH surely made up through contingent labor), we made sure that we never lost a search. In sum, we made progress.

By the end of my term, though, we knew we couldn't do much more because the backlash was so strong. We thought we were asking people to work a little harder so that we could get more tenure lines and cohabit a department with a more equitably distributed division of labor. In time, with more tenure lines to share service duties, etc., we even anticipated (rightly or wrongly, I don't know) that the workload would be lighter than before, not heavier. To some people, though, it just looked like we'd predictably turned into your typical administrator, insisting everyone do more under conditions in which they already felt overtaxed. To our everlasting surprise, our struggle to reverse adjunctification had made it appear in some eyes that *we* were the neoliberal Man squeezing the ordinary (TT and full-time NTT) Joe. Nobody embarks on projects expecting to end up a pariah in one's own neighborhood. Yet how critical it is, and how fortunate I am, that tenure gives some of us the ability to weather people's displeasure when we are convinced something is worth fighting for.

The students deserve a faculty who can make independent judgments. Let one anecdote stand as example. A professor came to me with an interesting question while I was chair. She'd been in a meeting to discuss our major's course requirements; the issue was whether or not we counted too many film classes toward the major. Unsurprisingly, opinion was divided. At a certain point, the "yes's"—too many film courses—had convinced the majority, but one of the "no's" was stubborn. Finally, this faculty member blurted, "Look, I am not on the tenure track and all I teach is film. You reduce the film courses students take and I may be out of a job!" The professor in my office asked, "Should we be thinking about our own employment when we decide on curriculum or strictly what we believe to be in the best interests of our students?" Obviously, the latter. We're not here to ensure our own futures but to help students prepare for theirs. Tenured faculty have the ability to make disinterested decisions to this end that other faculty, through no fault of their own, simply don't. This matters in university politics. It matters a lot and it matters often.

The tenure system acknowledges human nature—namely, the fact that people usually won't act against their own interests, regardless of the larger context. It takes this into account by enabling faculty to deliberate and research and teach and grade without anxiety over the next paycheck warping the outcome of these activities. We don't have to vote on curricular matters to gratify our supervisors, we don't have to deliver lab results that satisfy pharmaceutical companies, we don't have conference sponsored by TIAA-CREF (Teachers Insurance and Annuity Association—College Retirement Equities Fund), one in which there was no Karen Kelsky in attendance to puncture the self-serving rhetoric. Billed to administrators and higher education faculty as an opportunity to "envision faculty models of the future," it appears that the "faculty models" attendees were invited to "envision" were ones in which the tenure system plays a diminished, if not non-existent, role. The "more intentionality needed" in the title refers to more intentional hiring off the tenure track. Rather than accrue an off-track force as a groping-in-the-dark, defensive reaction to financial exigencies, the TIAA-CREF spokesperson encourages everyone to continue to employ adjuncts but to do it *intentionally*, strategically, proactively. On purpose. This bit of soft reportage by *Inside Higher Ed* gives the TIAA-CREF spokesperson the final word, as the conference itself probably did: "You do it [employ adjuncts] right," Paul Yaboski is quoted as saying, "and you're waving a trophy around."

In the bosom of such a conference, administrators freely admit that adjunct employment is "a key and permanent feature of their institutions' cost structure," in the words of SUNY vice chancellor for human resources Curtis Lloyd. That university budget officers now *count on* what was once a stop-gap measure is news to nobody. It wouldn't be news either to hear that someone had confessed this in a sheepish *what-are-you-gonna-do?* tone of voice. What's new is the idea that you might win a trophy for it and that you would wave that trophy around.

Thankfully, one conference participant experienced significant dissonance at this event. Valerie Martin Conley, chair of the department of counseling and higher education at Ohio University, is quoted as saying: "'Creeping into my head-scratching' is that 'if we take on creating policies around these individuals in these positions, it becomes much harder to ignore that we've devolved into that environment.... It sort of says it's O.K. to have them.'"[14] Professor Conley doesn't say she's "scratching her head" over the paradox that she's participating in working out policies for positions she never thought should exist in the first place. She says that this quantum reality is *creeping into* her *head-scratching.* Conley's syntax feels so honest because it reveals the unhappy movement from denial to disavowal when one begins to rationalize. Only unwelcome things *creep,* and they have to be very unwelcome to creep into our head only to be kicked back out to scratch it. She seems to be telling herself: *These positions exist. They suck (bad wages, no health benefits, invisibility in the university community). We once accepted their existence by telling ourselves that they were ad hoc, temporary, circumstantial. Now we must admit that these positions are permanently baked into our budgets. So even though we continue to believe in academic freedom and a significant degree of equality among faculty, and we know that an adjunct professoriate does not enjoy these intangible goods, we have to believe all the same that very modest improvements—like hiring with more intentionality, handing out adjunct faculty handbooks—can fix this problem.*

Adjunct faculty handbooks won't fix the problem, just as tarring all administrators with the same brush gets us nowhere. Last spring, Portland State faculty voted to authorize a strike. By the time a settlement had been reached, the union had prevented big cuts to academics. It had heavily relied, though, upon a rhetoric that demonized the very top for a rotten infrastructure that was many years in the rotting. Perhaps this was necessary to mobilize the faculty? I don't know, but I do know that many of us—those in union leadership, many members of senate, department chairs and senior faculty—had been here much longer than had either the president or provost. *We* had done as much—that is, nothing—about the quandary as they had. Caricaturing one or two people will not break down the system and rebuild it along more sustainable and ethical lines.

The reality that we all need to account for ourselves sunk in when I attended a forum held by the union in the final days of bargaining. The most dramatic testimony that night was given by someone who had been an adjunct at PSU for 13 years. He talked about the letters of recommendation he'd written over those years. Letters of recommendation—like so much else at the university—presume a stable faculty paid the kind of salary and given the kind of professional status that allows him or her to do many numbers of things without negotiating for a "wage" in return.

PSU hired this person term after term, paid him pennies, and relied upon him to write letters of recommendations for a *generation* of students. Our president had been here six years and the provost one and a half. They didn't even know this adjunct existed. Who did? The chair of the department he taught in. And if the tenure-track faculty in that department did not know he existed, they should have. The fact that this person was invisible was not one person's fault—but I will not invoke the agentless phrase "broken system" here. Real people wrote these contracts; real departments relied upon this labor. We can stop. The Appendix offers nuts-and-bolts advice for reform; the next chapter explains why tenure is an essential ingredient of that reform.

Notes

1. George Levine, "Putting the 'Literature' Back into Literature Departments," *ADE Bulletin* 113 (1996), p. 14.
2. Joe Berry, *Reclaiming the Ivory Tower: Organizing Adjuncts to Change Higher Education* (New York: Monthly Review Press, 2005), p. 7.
3. Allen Dunn, "Who Needs a Sociology of the Aesthetic? Freedom and Value in Bourdieu's *Rules of Art*," *boundary 2* 25.1 (1998), p. 90.
4. Julie Schumacher, *Dear Committee Members* (New York: Doubleday, 2014), p. 105.
5. Rosemary Feal, quoted in Elizabeth Segran, "The Adjunct Revolt: How Poor Professors Are Fighting Back," *The Atlantic* 28 Apr. 2014. http://www.theatlantic.com/business/archive/2014/04/the-adjunct-professor-crisis/361336/2/
6. Thomas Frank, "Congratulations, Class of 2014: You're Totally Screwed," *Salon* 18 May 2014. http://www.salon.com/2014/05/18/congratulations_class_of_2014_youre_totally_ screwed/

7. Louis Menand, ed., *The Future of Academic Freedom* (University of Chicago Press, 1996), p. 4.

8. Karen Kelsky, "Adjuncts, Assistant Professors, and a Broken Faculty Life Cycle," *The Professor Is In* (blog), 25 Jul. 2014. http://theprofessorisin.com/2014/07/25/adjuncts-assistant-professors-and-a-broken-faculty-life-cycle/

9. Marietta Del Favero and Nathaniel Bray, "The Faculty-Administrator Relationship: Partners in Prospective Governance?" *Scholar-Practitioner Quarterly* 3.1 (2005), p. 62.

10. George L. Mehaffy, "Challenge and Change," *Educause Review Online* 5 Sept. 2012. http://www.educause.edu/ero/article/challenge-and-change

11. "The Digital Degree," *The Economist* 28 Jun. 2104. http://www.economist.com/news/briefing/21605899-staid-higher-education-business-about-experience-welcome-earthquake-digital. The Moody's official quoted is Susan Fitzgerald.

12. Robert Poch, *Academic Freedom in American Higher Education: Rights, Responsibilities, and Limitations* (San Francisco: Jossey-Bass, 1993), p. xv.

13. David Perry, "Faculty Refuse to See Themselves as Workers. Why?," *Chronicle of Higher Education*, Vitae *blog*, 22 May 2104. https://chroniclevitae.com/news/509-faculty-refuse-to-see-themselves-as-workers-why

14. Colleen Flaherty, "More 'Intentionality' Needed," *Inside Higher Ed* 23 Jun. 2014. https://www.insidehighered.com/news/2014/06/23/discussion-focuses-envisioning-faculty-models-future

that public employees can be protected by the First Amendment if their statements have no credibility whatsoever, following the precedent of Pickering v. Board of Education (1968). As Michael's MLA statement phrased it, "faculty members whose statements are utterly ill-considered and misinformed enjoy First Amendment protection from administrative retaliation, but faculty members who know what they're talking about speak up at their peril."[14]

This heightened uncertainty, coupled with the deprofessionalization that ad hoc hiring amounts to, poisons cultures of shared governance. In a predominantly tenure-track context, by contrast, the freedom one experiences among one's peers was never far from the reality when participating in shared governance. This version just didn't achieve distinct articulation. Was this because at the time the ideal was developed—the 1930s and 1940s—an emphasis on a community defined by equality might have raised the specter of communism and provoked political resistance? More likely, this alternative understanding of academic freedom went unrealized because we moderns have a hard time conceiving of freedom as necessarily plural and collective rather than defensively singular and individual. Whereas a professional version of academic freedom might have emphasized the necessity of building and maintaining a politically guaranteed and horizontal space for its exercise, the negative version of academic freedom emphasizes the autonomy of individuals. These individuals are more likely to interfere with one another than to be the condition of one another's freedom. It's as if once we realized that we needed the professor to have autonomy from overt agents of power (the board, the state, the market), we began to believe, if only half-consciously, that he should have autonomy from everybody—even his peers. Rather, as sociologist Craig Calhoun writes, professors "should be seen as obligated to carry out their work in a sufficiently public way for it to be judged by the relevant professional community."[15]

From 1940 on, a negative version of academic freedom (freedom *from*) dominated the academy, and the internal organization of faculty deliberation was typically neglected. Negative freedom prepares a mind for "idle curiosity," in Thorstein Veblen's memorable phrase from *The Higher Learning in America*. Today tenured professors avoid this phrase for good reason—the idea of idleness does not market well in this market—but we still take the point: we can't know in advance what discoveries or concepts will yield value for society, and so knowledge must be an end in itself. But "idle curiosity" is clearly the experience of the (singular) person thinking, someone in friendly conversation with him or herself. One imagines a person alone—or, rather, someone in that state Socrates calls "the two in one" that every human being becomes when he or she is thinking. "Idle curiosity" does not lead us to visualize a plurality. We don't picture the Faculty Senate debating the promises and perils of online technology or the Third Estate pounding out the Tennis Court Oath at the start of the French Revolution.

We can no longer think about academic freedom in only or even primarily individual terms, because the three-tiered faculty workforce has changed the once-horizontal space of governance into an uncomfortably hierarchical one. The nature of the *space* of governance has changed. When the professoriate engaged in governance and service was overwhelmingly tenured or tenure-track, it did not spend a lot of time worrying about internal conflicts of interest and the subtle or not-so-subtle pull of hierarchy. Senior faculty and junior faculty were aware, of course, of the power differential between them. But the idea that someone deliberating on the English major might be unable to cover his or her cost of living the following year if the committee decided to eliminate the popular culture or the pre-1800 literature requirement—this had not occurred often enough to register, not even in the retrenchment years of the early 1970s.

We haven't taken into account that the structural transformation of the professoriate entailed a massive loss of academic freedom. "For 75 percent of instructors in higher education, it is meaningless to claim that they possess academic freedom in

4 On the Rails

Jennifer Ruth and Michael Bérubé

Michael:

The national leaders in the fight for contingent faculty rights are not well known. This is no surprise: we are talking about the leaders of loose coalitions of (mostly) unorganized and invisible faculty members, people unseen and unacknowledged even (or especially) by their own nominal departmental colleagues in the tenured ranks. It is only in the last two or three years that they have begun to become visible—and audible—as advocates for reform in higher education. Only rarely does the mainstream media (that is, outside the confines of the higher-ed press) feature the perspective of adjunct faculty: we can point to a *New York Times* story on J. D. Hoff of CUNY, a pair of PBS stories by (now former) adjunct professor Joe Fruscione, a searing *Washington Post* editorial ("Adjunct Professors Fight for Crumbs on Campus") by Colman McCarthy, and of course the coverage of the life and death of Margaret Mary Vojtko.[1] But we are counting on the fingers of one hand here. Very few people outside the precincts of academe know of the work of Joe Berry, president of the Coalition of Contingent Academic Labor (COCAL) and author of *Reclaiming the Ivory Tower*; or Maria Maisto, president of the New Faculty Majority (NFM); or Robert Samuels, president of the University of California-American Federation of Teachers and author of *Why Public Higher Education Should Be Free*; or Robin Sowards (also on the board of the NFM), who helped lead the fight to organize adjunct faculty at Duquesne as part of the Adjunct Faculty Association, affiliated (as is appropriate for Pittsburgh) with the

121

United Steelworkers of America. But we know of their work, and you should too. Much of what we argue in this book has been inspired by them, by precept and by example.

In 2012, thanks in part to his own ingenuity and in part to the wonders of the internet, Josh Boldt, then a young adjunct faculty member at the University of Georgia, suddenly joined the ranks of these unseen and unsung leaders. After reading my report on the January 2012 summit meeting of the New Faculty Majority in Washington,[2] which discussed the Modern Language Association's wage recommendations for contingent faculty (at the time, $6800/course), Boldt created "The Adjunct Project," an online crowdsourcing device that allowed contingent-faculty members to upload the details of their employment contracts—anonymously. The idea, of course, was that The Adjunct Project would reveal how many institutions (spoiler alert: *nearly all*) were falling short of MLA recommendations. As Boldt wrote:

> Almost $7K per course! Most adjuncts have never seen anything close to that figure. I personally have taught at schools that pay right at or below $2000 maximum per course. Feel free to do the math on that one (Hint: a 5/5 pays $20,000 annually). You can be a terrible human being and still recognize that a full-time teacher should earn much more than that. Just in case you're not familiar with the usual procedure, full-time professors generally teach much less than 10 courses per year. Some teach as few as three. The MLA's recommendation is based on the assumption of a 3/3 teaching load, which sounds about perfect. I would venture to say most adjuncts would agree. Three courses per semester is ideal because it allows teaching to be the primary focus (as it should be), and it also permits some time for research and professional development. So, about $40,000 a year. That isn't too much to ask I don't think. Especially considering all adjuncts have advanced degrees in their fields....

Table 1 Salary minimums for Portland State faculty members, 2014–15

Rank	9-month appt. 1 Feb. 2014	12-month appt. 1 Jan. 2014
Professor	$80,748	$98,520
Clinical or Professor of Practice	80,748	98,520
Associate Professor	65,637	80,088
Associate Clinical or Professor of Practice	65,637	80,088
Assistant Professor	54,918	67,008
Assistant Clinical Professor or Professor of Practice	54,918	67,008
Senior Instructor II	53,820	65,664
Senior Instructor I	45,603	55,644
Instructor	40,005	48,816
Senior Research Associate II	49,554	60,456
Senior Research Associate I	45,774	55,848
Research Associate	43,812	53,472
Senior Research Assistant II	42,733	52,140
Senior Research Assistant I	40,698	49,656
Research Assistant	40,005	48,816

model or something very much like it. Administrators who have experienced the kind of strife we experienced recently at Portland State are more likely to be open to such proposals. At institutions where top administrators have yet to apprehend the way stepped-up union activity has changed the game, Faculty Senates will be the place to articulate and push through similar plans. A number of Faculty Senates have already been very active on this front. (See the Senate webpages for University of Colorado at Boulder—in particular, their Final Task Force Report of 2010—and the University of Oregon.)

Jennifer and Michael:

Finally, we must say a word about the pain that is inevitable in our proposal for reform. There are a lot of bad reasons why administrators and TT faculty have done nothing about the crisis, and why the burden of change has fallen too heavily on the activism of the least-empowered faculty group. We've talked about many of these bad reasons in this book. There is, however, one *good* reason why the empowered constituencies have done so little even when they have not been paralyzed or fatalistic: because any considered and sustainable change is unlikely to accommodate all the individuals who by rights deserve to be accommodated. It turns out that bucking the system that is already in place is going to be almost as hard on the conscience as maintaining it is. Even if in the long run better jobs with access to tenure are created, and this improves the university (and, in turn, society) by strengthening academic freedom, particular persons will lose out. No matter how ingenious the circumstances designed to move us from a majority off-track to majority on-track workforce, no matter how irreproachably conscientious, there will be outcomes that feel—and undoubtedly are—unjust from one perspective or another.

The proposal in the Appendix makes it possible for many NTT faculty to be converted to a teaching-intensive tenure track, and as we eliminate NTT positions, we advocate replacing them with TT hires in regional or national searches. The NTT faculty who were hired ad hoc will be eligible to apply for those positions—but inevitably, those faculty members who do not possess terminal degrees will be at a disadvantage in such searches, which will of course draw many applicants (regionally or nationally) with terminal degrees, including those people with terminal degrees who already work as adjunct instructors at the institutions. We expect, therefore, that our proposal will be seen in some quarters as elitist, privileging PhD holders over the legions of MAs and ABDs (people who have completed all requirements but for their dissertations) now occupying NTT positions. Our proposal does indeed privilege PhD holders. But this is not elitism; it is *professionalism*. Marc Bousquet puts it well in *How the University Works*: when "degree holding no longer represents control over who may practice," the result is "a failed monopoly of professional labor."[11] As

Kelsky, Karen. "Adjuncts, Assistant Professors, and a Broken Faculty Life Cycle," *The Professor Is In* (blog), 25 Jul. 2014. http://theprofessor isin.com/2014/07/25/adjuncts-assistant-professors-and-a-broken-faculty-life-cycle/

Kermode, Frank. "The Academy vs. the Humanities," *Atlantic Monthly* Aug. 1997. http://www.theatlantic.com/past/docs/issues/97aug/academy.htm

Kernan, Alvin. *The Death of Literature.* New Haven: Yale University Press, 1992.
——— ed. *What's Happened to the Humanities?* Princeton University Press, 1997.

Kimball, Roger. "The Periphery v. the Center: The MLA in Chicago," *New Criterion* 9.6 (Feb. 1991). http://www.newcriterion.com/articles.cfm/The-periphery-vs—the-center—the-MLA-in-Chicago-5411

Kittay, Eva Feder. *Love's Labor: Essays on Women, Equality, and Dependency.* New York: Routledge, 1999.

Klinkenborg, Verlyn. "The Decline and Fall of the English Major," *New York Times* 22 Jun. 2013. http://www.nytimes.com/2013/06/23/opinion/sunday/the-decline-and-fall-of-the-english-major.html?_r=0

Kovalik, Daniel. "Death of an Adjunct," *Pittsburgh Post-Gazette* 18 Sept. 2013. http://www.post-gazette.com/opinion/Op-Ed/2013/09/18/Death-of-an-adjunct/stories/201309180224

Landers, Elizabeth. "Contingent Labor: National Perspectives, Local Solutions," *Profession 2013.* http://profession.commons.mla.org/2013/10/08/contingent-labor-national-perspectives-local-solutions/

Laurence, David. "A Profile of the Non-Tenure-Track Academic Workforce," *ADE (Association of Departments of English) Bulletin* 153 (2014): 6–22.

Leatherman, Courtney, and Robin Wilson. "Embittered by a Bleak Job Market, Graduate Students Take on the MLA," 18 Dec. 1998. https://chronicle.com/article/Embittered-by-a-Bleak-Job/30852

Lehman, David. *Signs of the Times: Deconstruction and the Fall of Paul de Man.* New York: Poseidon Press, 1991.

Leo, John. "Campus Life, Fully Exposed," *U.S. News and World Report* 10 Jan. 2005. Rpt. http://wesleyanargus.com/2005/01/25/campus-life-fully-exposed/

Levi, Edward H. *Point of View: Talks on Education.* University of Chicago Press, 1970.

Levine, George. "Putting the 'Literature' Back into Literature Departments," *ADE Bulletin* 113 (1996): 13–20.

Longmate, Jack, and Frank Cosco. *Program for Change: 2010–2030.* Revised, 2013. http://vccfa.ca/newsite/wp-content/uploads/2012/05/Access-the-Program-for-Change-May-2013.pdf

Marshall, Thurgood. "Remarks of Thurgood Marshall at the Annual Seminar of the San Francisco Patent and Trade Law Association,"

Maui, Hawaii, 6 May 1987. http://www.thurgoodmarshall.com/speeches/constitutional_speech.htm

McCarthy, Colman. "Adjunct Professors Fight for Crumbs on Campus," *Washington Post* 22 Aug. 2014. http://www.washingtonpost.com/opinions/adjunct-professors-fight-for-crumbs-on-campus/2014/08/22/ca92eb38-28b1-11e4-8593-da634b334390_story.html

McMahan, Jeff. "Cognitive Disability and Cognitive Enhancement." In Eva Feder Kittay and Licia Carlson, eds, *Cognitive Disability and its Challenge to Moral Philosophy*. Boston: Wiley-Blackwell, 2010. 345–367.
——— "Cognitive Disability, Misfortune, and Justice," *Philosophy and Public Affairs* 25.1 (1996): 3–35.
——— *The Ethics of Killing: Problems at the Margins of Life*. Oxford University Press, 2003.

Mehaffy, George L. "Challenge and Change," *Educause Review Online* 5 Sept. 2012. http://www.educause.edu/ero/article/challenge-and-change

Menand, Louis, ed. *The Future of Academic Freedom*. University of Chicago Press, 1996.
——— *The Metaphysical Club: A Story of Ideas in America*. New York: Farrar, Straus and Giroux, 2001.

Meranze, Michael. "We Wish We Weren't in Kansas Anymore: An Elegy for Academic Freedom," *Los Angeles Review of Books* 4 Mar. 2014. http://lareviewofbooks.org/essay/wish-werent-kansas-anymore-elegy-academic-freedom

Nelson, Cary. *No University is an Island: Saving Academic Freedom*. New York University Press, 2010.

Newfield, Christopher. *Unmaking the Public University: The Forty-Year Assault on the Middle Class*. Cambridge, MA: Harvard University Press, 2008.

Nussbaum, Martha. *Frontiers of Justice: Disability, Nationality, Species Membership*. Cambridge, MA: Harvard University Press, 2006.

Patton, Stacey. "The Ph.D. Now Comes with Food Stamps." *Chronicle of Higher Education* 6 May 2012. http://chronicle.com/article/From-Graduate-School-to/131795/

Perry, David. "Faculty Refuse to See Themselves as Workers. Why?" *Chronicle of Higher Education,* Vitae *blog,* 22 May 2104. https://chroniclevitae.com/news/509-faculty-refuse-to-see-themselves-as-workers-why

Poch, Robert. *Academic Freedom in American Higher Education: Rights, Responsibilities, and Limitations*. San Francisco: Jossey-Bass, 1993.

Post, Robert. "The Structure of Academic Freedom." In Beshara Doumani, ed., *Academic Freedom after September 11*. New York: Zone Books, 2006.

Professional Employment Practices for Non-Tenure-Track Faculty Members: Recommendations and Evaluative Questions. MLA Committee on

Contingent Labor in the Profession. New York: Modern Language Association, 2011. http://www.mla.org/pdf/clip_stmt_final_may11.pdf

"Ramifications of the Supreme Court's Ruling in Garcetti v. Ceballos," Modern Language Association Committee on Academic Freedom and Professional Rights and Responsibilities. http://www.mla.org/garcetti_ceballos

Rawls, John. *A Theory of Justice.* Cambridge, MA: Harvard University Press, 1971.

Readings, Bill. *The University in Ruins.* Cambridge, MA: Harvard University Press, 1996.

Robbins, Bruce. "Outside Pressures," *Works and Days* 51/52, 53/54 (2008–9): 339–345.

Russo, Richard. *Straight Man.* New York: Vintage, 1997.

Ruth, Jennifer. *Novel Professions: Interested Disinterest and the Making of the Professional in the Victorian Novel.* Columbus: Ohio State University Press, 2006.

——— "What Can We Do Now that Adjunct Sections are Written Into Universities' Fiscal Survival Strategy?" *Remaking the University* 22 Jul. 2014. http://utotherescue.blogspot.com/2014/07/what-can-we-do-now-that-adjunct.html

——— "When Tenure-Track Faculty Take on the Problem of Adjunctification," *Remaking the University* 25 May 2013. http://utotherescue.blogspot.com/2013/05/when-tenure-track-faculty-take-on.html

——— "Why Are Faculty Complicit in Creating a Disposable Workforce?" *Remaking the University* 13 Jul. 2014. http://utotherescue.blogspot.com/2014/07/why-are-faculty-complicit-in-creating.html

Samuels, Robert. *Why Public Higher Education Should Be Free: How to Decrease Cost and Increase Quality at American Universities.* New Brunswick, NJ: Rutgers University Press, 2013.

Schmidt, Ben. "A Crisis in the Humanities?" *Chronicle of Higher Education* 10 Jun. 2013. http://chronicle.com/blognetwork/edgeofthewest/2013/06/10/the-humanities-crisis/

Schmidt, Peter. "New Complaint to Accreditor Assails College's Treatment of Adjuncts," *Chronicle of Higher Education* 17 Apr. 2013. http://chronicle.com/article/New-Complaint-to-Accreditor/138555

Schumacher, Julie. *Dear Committee Members.* New York: Doubleday, 2014.

Scott, Joan Wallach. "Knowledge, Power, and Academic Freedom," *Social Research* 76.2 (2009): 451–480.

Segran, Elizabeth. "The Adjunct Revolt: How Poor Professors Are Fighting Back," *Atlantic* 28 Apr. 2014. http://www.theatlantic.com/business/archive/2014/04/the-adjunct-professor-crisis/361336/2/

Silver, Nate. "As More Attend College, Majors Become More Career-Focused," *New York Times* 25 Jun. 2013. http://fivethirtyeight.blogs.nytimes.com/2013/06/25/as-more-attend-college-majors-become-more-career-focused

Singer, Peter. *Rethinking Life and Death: The Collapse of our Traditional Ethics*. New York: St. Martin's, 1994.

—— "Speciesism and Moral Status." In Eva Feder Kittay and Licia Carlson, eds, *Cognitive Disability and its Challenge to Moral Philosophy*. Boston: Wiley-Blackwell, 2010. 331–344.

Small, Helen. *The Value of the Humanities*. Oxford University Press, 2013.

Smith, Barbara Herrnstein. *Contingencies of Value: Alternative Perspectives for Critical Theory*. Cambridge, MA: Harvard University Press, 1988.

Staton, Michael. "The Degree is Doomed," *Harvard Business Review HBR Blog Network*, 8 Jan. 2014. http://blogs.hbr.org/2014/01/the-degree-is-doomed/

Swarns, Rachel L. "Crowded Out of Ivory Tower, Adjuncts See a Life Less Lofty," *New York Times* 19 Jan. 2014. http://www.nytimes.com/2014/01/20/nyregion/crowded-out-of-ivory-tower-adjuncts-see-a-life-less-lofty.html?_r=0

The Teaching of the Arts and Humanities at Harvard College: Mapping the Future. http://artsandhumanities.fas.harvard.edu/files/humanities/files/mapping_the_future_31_may_2013.pdf

Tenure and Teaching-Intensive Appointments. Washington, DC: American Association of University Professors, 2009. http://www.aaup.org/report/tenure-and-teaching-intensive-appointments

Veblen, Thorstein. *The Higher Learning in America: A Memorandum on the Conduct of Universities by Business Men*. New York: Cosimo, 2005 [1904].

Index

Bold entries refer to figures or tables.

academic freedom, 24
  contingent faculty, 12, 15, 104
  "Declaration of Principles
    on Academic Freedom and
    Academic Tenure" (1915),
    101–102, 113
  different conceptions of, 87–88
  Garcetti v. Ceballos (United
    States Supreme Court),
    107–109
  loss of, 110–111
  negative version of, 106–107,
    109–110
  as paradoxical principle, 114
  as a professional freedom,
    101–102, 105, 109, 116
  radical nature of, 114
  reconceptualized in terms of
    rights, 104–105
  shared governance, 89, 107,
    114
  tenure system, 101–103,
    114–115
academic infighting, 89–90
accountability
  administration/administrators,
    80
  tenured faculty, 75–76, 127,
    128
  universities, 138
activism of contingent faculty,
    62–64, 121–124, 125
  attitudes toward tenure,
    124–125

Adjunct Action, 63
adjunct faculty, 13
  invisibility of, 16
  lack of stake in institutions,
    88
  original function of, 17
  as permanent feature, 83
  wages, 60–61, 122–123
  years spent teaching, 16–17
  see also contingent faculty
Adjunct Faculty Association,
    121–122
Adjunct Project, 122–123
administration/administrators
  accountability, 80
  attitudes toward tenure, 78–79,
    80
  denial over contingent faculty
    system, 130
  expansion of, 22, 76–77
  pressures on, 79, 82
  tensions with faculty, 79,
    82
Albert, David, 51
American Academy of Arts and
    Sciences, *The Heart of the
    Matter*, 1
American Association of
    University Professors, 12, 13,
    24–25, 135
  "Declaration of Principles
    on Academic Freedom and
    Academic Tenure" (1915),
    101–102, 113

American Association of University
    Professors – *continued*
    *The Inclusion in Governance
    of Faculty Members Holding
    Contingent Appointments*, 111,
    112, 113, 115, 118
    "On the Relationship of Faculty
    Governance to Academic
    Freedom," 107
    "Statement of Principles on
    Academic Freedom and
    Tenure" (1940), 102, 106
    *Tenure and Teaching-Intensive
    Appointments*, 88, 117, 126,
    129–130
American Federation of Teachers
    (AFT), 63
Amnesty International, 36
Anderson, Amanda, 38
animal rights, 34, 40, 45, 46
Arendt, Hannah, 102, 103, 114,
    117–118
Aronowitz, Stanley, 57

Bauerlein, Mark, 2
Baynton, Douglas, 47
Benhabib, Seyla, 35
Berlin, Isaiah, 106
Berry, Joe, 60, 88, 121
Bok, Derek, 127–128
Boldt, Josh, 81, 122–123, 124–125
Bousquet, Marc, 16, 20, 57, 129,
    134–135
Brooks, David, 1–2
Burgan, Mary, 89
Butler, Judith, 34
    universalism, 35–37, 38

Calhoun, Craig, 109
Ceballos, Richard, 107–108
Chace, William M., 2, 3–4
Coalition of Contingent Academic
    Labor (COCAL), 121

cognitive capacity, 40, 45
    and moral status, 43–44, 45–46
Cohen, Patricia, 27
Conley, Valerie Martin, 83–84
contingency, 33–34
    contextual nature of value, 33
    human rights, 34
contingent faculty, 12, 13
    attitudes toward tenure, 104,
        124–125
    converting to teaching-
        intensive tenured positions,
        19–20: evaluation for tenure,
        149; evaluation of teaching,
        147; impact of reform on,
        136, 144–145; Portland
        State University, 142–148;
        privileging of PhD holders,
        134–135; service workload,
        148
    costs of reform, 134
    courseloads, 91–92
    dependence on department
        head, 88
    as employment choice, 18–19
    expansion of, 111
    failed strategy of converting to
        tenure lines, 67–69
    "freeway flyers," 18
    growth across disciplines,
        129–130
    ineligibility for unemployment
        benefits, 15
    institutional designation of, 17
    lack of academic freedom, 12,
        15, 104
    need for reform of hiring
        process, 94–95
    not treated as professionals,
        130–131
    number of, 14
    participation in governance:
        consequences of, 112; erosion

of tenure, 99–101; problems
with, 115–116; weak position
in, 98–99, 111–112
patronage systems, 92–93, 94
perceptions of, 17
powerlessness of, 123
precarious position of, 18, 103
problems with reforming
non-tenure track policy, 95–98
shared governance, 101
tenure as long-term solution
for, 126
unequal access to promotion,
95–96
wages, 14–15, 17, 122–123
see also activism of contingent
faculty; adjunct faculty
Cosco, Frank, 139n
Cross, John, 90
cultural capital, devaluation of,
58–59
culture wars, 8–9

decision-making, academic, 95
contingent faculty's
participation in, 98, 101
"Declaration of Principles on
Academic Freedom and
Academic Tenure" (1915),
101–102, 113
Delbanco, Andrew, 4–5, 27, 28
de Man, Paul, 51
democracy, 101, 115
deprofessionalization of college
teaching, 11, 14
activism in combating, 62–64,
121–124
consequences of, 11–12, 70–71
impact on graduate programs, 16
inertia of tenured faculty,
64–71: advantages of adjunct
hiring, 66–67; feelings of
helplessness, 64–65; hoping

to convert to tenure lines,
67–69; innocence of, 66;
institutional costs, 69–71;
personal costs, 69
tenure as long-term solution
for, 126
Deresiewicz, William, 49–50, 137
Dewey, John, 114
disability studies
cognitive capacity, 44, 45
Down syndrome, 40–43
general relevance of, 47–48
inequality, 47
philosophy's silence on
disability, 40
universalism, 39
doctorate (PhD), *see* terminal
degrees
Down syndrome, 40–43

Enlightenment
critique of, 30, 32–33
as incomplete project, 38
universality, 30

Feal, Rosemary, 64
Fish, Stanley, 51
Frank, Thomas, 71, 76
"freeway flyers," 18
Fruscione, Joe, 121

Gerber, Larry, 101, 107, 115
Giroux, Henry, 79
Goldenberg, Edie, 90
governance
contingent faculty's participation
in, 12: consequences of, 112;
erosion of tenure, 99–101;
problems with, 115–116; weak
position of, 98–99, 111–112
tenured faculty's participation
in, 75, 77
see also shared governance

graduate programs, impact of
   deprofessionalization, 16
Green River Community College,
   98–99
Greenstadt, Amy, 14, 132
Guillory, John, 58, 59, 60, 61

Habermas, Jürgen, 37–38, 40
Hall, Tamron, 2
Harvard, 7
Harvey, David, 58
Heraclitus, 30
higher education, 138–139
   achievements of American
      system, 137–138
   decline in funding of, 15–16, 22
   erosion of, 138
   inequality in, 24
   university's mission, 24–25
hiring of faculty
   expansion of non-tenure
      faculty, 90–91
   fast-tracked hiring, 91
   growth of patronage system,
      92–93, 94
   inequality in courseloads, 91–92
   need to reform contingent
      faculty hiring, 94–95:
      problems with, 95–98
   teaching-intensive tenure
      track, 146–147: evaluation of
      teaching, 147
   tenured faculty, 93, 94
   terminal degrees, 19–20,
      134–135
   three-tiered system, 90
   unprofessional practices,
      19, 20
Hoeller, Keith, 98–99
Hoff, J. D., 121
homophobia, 34–35
House Committee on Education
   and the Workforce, 63

humanities
   attacks on current practices in,
      3, 4–5, 14, 49–50
   aversion to timelessness and
      universality, 29, 30
   calls for justification of, 27–28
   decline in tenure-track jobs, 10,
      15, 60
   decline narrative, 1–5, 7:
      reasons for, 9–10
   degrees as percentage of all
      degrees, 4
   degrees as percentage of
      college-age population, 6
   employment crisis, 58
   impact of socio-economic
      changes, 58, 59–60, 61
   increase in degrees awarded in,
      5–7
   justification of, 51–54
   public image of, 50–51
   self-inflicted wounds, 49, 50–51
   stability of undergraduate
      enrollments, 7–8
   traditional justification for, 29
human rights, contingent nature
   of, 34

ideology, claims of universality,
   30
inequality
   disability, 47
   higher education, 24
Instructor Bill of Rights, 103, 111

Jameson, Fredric, 30
Johnson, Barbara, 51

Kelsky, Karen, 78–79
Kennedy, Anthony, 108
Kermode, Frank, 5
Kezar, Adrianna, 130
Kimball, Roger, 34

Kittay, Eva, 39, 40
Klinkenborg, Verlyn, 7
Kronman, Arthur, 27

Landers, Elizabeth, 123, 136
Lehman, David, 33
Leo, John, 34
Levi, Edward, 23–24
Levine, George, 58–59, 60
literary studies, attacks on current
    practices in, 49–50
Lloyd, Curtis, 83
Longmate, Jack, 139n
Lovejoy, Arthur, 101–102, 114
Lyotard, Jean-François, 37, 38

Maisto, Maria, 63, 121, 123
managerial staff, expansion of, 22
Marshall, Thurgood, 30, 31–32, 40
McCarthy, Colman, 121
McMahan, Jeff, 43–44, 45–46, 47
Menand, Louis, 75, 93, 116
Meranze, Michael, 12, 88,
    110–111
Miller, George, 63
modernity, as incomplete project,
    40
Modern Language Association
    (MLA), 12, 17, 63, 107, 122,
    123, 135
    *Professional Employment Practices
    for Non-Tenure Track Faculty
    Members*, 131–132
moral status, and cognitive
    capacity, 43–44, 45–46

National Center for Education
    Statistics, 7
National Study of Postsecondary
    Faculty, 16
Nelson, Cary, 57, 77, 114
New Faculty Majority (NFM), 63,
    121, 122–123

Newfield, Christopher, 8–9, 12
Nussbaum, Martha, 39

Oakley, Francis C., 27

Part-Time Worker Bill of Rights
    Act (2013), 63
patronage systems, 89, 115–116
    growth of, 92–93, 94
peer review
    teaching-intensive tenured
        positions, 19
    tenured faculty, 13, 17, 88
Penn State University, 13
Perry, David, 81
philosophy, and disability, 40
Poch, Robert, 80
political correctness, 34
Portland State University (PSU),
    14, 84–85
    Ad Hoc Committee on NTT
        Faculty Policy, 95–96, 128
    casualization of faculty, 129
    Curriculum Committee, 96–97
    implementing teaching-intensive
        tenure track, 142–148:
        evaluation for tenure, 148;
        evaluation of teaching, 147,
        148; hiring process, 146–147;
        impact on contingent faculty,
        144–145; reasons for, 143–144
    problems with reforming non-
        tenure track policy, 95–98
    salary minimums, 132, **133**
Poston, Muriel, 130
Post, Robert, 104–105, 114
private universities, increase in
    tuition costs, 22
privatization, impact on public
    universities, 8–9
professional associations, combating
    deprofessionalization, 63
promotion, unequal access to, 95–96

public universities
distinctive features of, 8–9
increase in tuition costs, 15,
21–22
loss of trust in, 71
see also higher education

queer theory, 34–35

Rawls, John, 39
Reading, Bill, 57
Reed, Adolph, Jr., 39
Re, Kathryn, 98
relativism, 33
Robbins, Bruce, 116
Ross, Andrew, 51
Ruhl, Nathan, 129–130
Russo, Richard, 65

Samuels, Robert, 121, 123
Schmid, Julie, 57
Schmidt, Ben, 5–6
Schumacher, Julie, 62, 64–65
Scott, Joan, 116
Sedgwick, Eve, 34
Seligman, Edwin, 101–102
Service Employees International
Union (SEIU), 63
shared governance, 77–78
academic freedom, 89, 107, 114
academic infighting, 89–90
deterioration of, 89
equality through organization,
114
rewarding nature of, 106
tensions in, 79
tenured faculty, 101–103
see also governance
Silver, Nate, 5
Sinclair, Upton, 112
Singer, Peter, 40–41, 42, 43–44, 47
Small, Helen, 11
Smith, Barbara Herrnstein, 30, 33

social constructionism, 42–43
social contract tradition, critique
of, 39
Sokal hoax, 51
Souter, David, 108
Sowards, Robin, 121
speciesism, 44
student debt, 22, 71

teaching-intensive tenure track,
19
benefits of, 75–76
costs of reform, 134
evaluation for tenure, 148
evaluation of teaching, 147
hiring process, 146–147
impact of reform on contingent
faculty, 136, 144–145
local variations in reform
process, 136–137
need for, 129–130
privileging of PhD holders,
19–20, 134–135
proposal for implementation
at Portland State University,
142–148
reasons for, 143–144
service workload, 148
tenured faculty/system
academic freedom, 101–103,
114–115
accountability, 75–76, 127,
128
contingent faculty's attitude
toward, 104, 124–125
courseloads, 91
decline in, 10, 15, 60
defense of, 127–128
empowerment of, 126–127
equality, 90, 117
erosion of tenure, 99–101
expansion through changes in
division of labor, 72–74

hiring process, 93, 94
independence, 72, 74–75, 117–118, 126–127
inertia in face of deprofessionalization, 64–71: advantages of adjunct hiring, 66–67; denial over, 130; feelings of helplessness, 64–65; hoping to convert to tenure lines, 67–69; innocence over, 66; institutional costs, 69–71; personal costs, 69
institutional designation of, 17–18
as long-term solution for contingent faculty, 126
opposition to tenure system, 23, 127
participation in university governance, 75
peer review, 13, 17, 88
professional identity, 82
public's view of, 71
responsibilities of, 82
self-perceptions, 81–82
tensions with administrators, 79, 80, 82
tenure as legitimating concept, 75, 93, 113–114
see also teaching-intensive tenure track
terminal degrees
alleged overproduction of PhDs, 16
hiring of faculty, 19–20
privileging holders of, 134–135
underhiring of PhDs, 135
TIAA-CREF (Teachers Insurance and Annuity Association—College Retirement Equities Fund), 83

timelessness
critique of, 29, 30
ideological motives, 30
tuition costs, 15, 20–21

undergraduate enrollment, growth in, 15
United States Constitution, 30–32
United States Supreme Court, and Garcetti v. Ceballos, 107–109
universality
critique of, 29, 30
disputes over boundaries of, 47
Enlightenment, 32–33
ideological motives, 30
as incomplete project, 38–39
Judith Butler on, 35–37, 38
openness to challenge, 40, 46–47
poststructuralist critique of, 46–47
University of California-American Federation of Teachers, 121

value, contextual nature of, 33
Vancouver Plan, 139n
Veblen, Thorstein, 110
visual and performing arts, degrees awarded, 6–7
Vojtko, Margaret Mary, 16–17, 121

wages
adjunct faculty, 60–61
Adjunct Project, 122–123
contingent faculty, 14–15, 122–123
minimum recommendations, 17
Portland State faculty, 132, **133**
Vancouver Plan, 139n
Warner, Michael, 34

Yaboski, Paul, 83
Yale, 7

CPSIA information can be obtained at www.ICGtesting.com
Printed in the USA
LVOW10s1749280116

472729LV00011B/138/P